Embroidered

Childhood MEMORIES

Brenna Hopkins & Nori Koenig

American Quilter's Society
P. O. Box 3290 • Paducah, KY 42002-3290
www.AQSquilt.com

Located in Paducah, Kentucky, the American Quilter's Society (AQS) is dedicated to promoting the accomplishments of today's quilters. Through its publications and events, AQS strives to honor today's quiltmakers and their work and to inspire future creativity and innovation in quiltmaking.

EDITOR: SHELLEY L. HAWKINS
GRAPHIC DESIGN: ELAINE WILSON
COVER DESIGN: MICHAEL BUCKINGHAM
PHOTOGRAPHY: CHARLES R. LYNCH

Library of Congress Cataloging-in-Publication Data

Hopkins, Brenna.
    Embroidered childhood memories / by Brenna Hopkins & Nori Koenig.
    p. cm.
    ISBN 1-57432-792-5
    1. Embroidery--Patterns.   2. Crib quilts--United States.   3.
Children's quilts--United States.   I. Koenig, Nori. II. Title.
TT775.H67 2002
746.46'041--dc21

2002000906

Additional copies of this book may be ordered from the American Quilter's Society, PO Box 3290, Paducah, KY 42002-3290, or online at www.AQSquilt.com.

Acknowledgments

This book has something in common with the long since grown-up babies who once slept underneath quilts with these designs. It started as a gleam in someone's eye. Nori Koenig knows adorable when she sees it, and her tenacity and persistence guarantee that, sooner or later, others will see it too. Her mom, Carol Schmitt, had something to do with that. It's in Carol's memory that Nori kept stitching through thick and thin, and it seems likely that Carol's patient, guiding hand is still helping us both.

Brenna

After the gleam comes the hard work, and there are no two people to whom we are more indebted than editors *Shelley Hawkins* and *Barbara Smith*. Where they get their supply of patience and good humor is a mystery, but apparently, there is an inexhaustible well. Our appreciation for their efforts cannot be overstated. Thank you from the bottom of our hearts.

Maureen DeLorme and *Lynn Hanke* gave us invaluable help testing the designs and projects.

Craig and *Al* both found their own ways to live with women who are more likely to present them with finished quilt blocks than dinner when they get home.

Miss Pam knows that without her wisely mischievous counsel, her sister would accomplish much less.

Glenda, Laura, Pauline, and *Billie* never failed to insist that this crazy collecting made perfect sense to them, so at least we were not alone in our madness.

And we have to thank *Doyle* and *Lu,* and especially *Effie,* again and again, because without them, none of this would have happened.

It's no exaggeration to say that every stitcher who has visited our booth or ordered from our catalog has had some hand in this book. Their encouragement enticed us toward our own dreams, with microscopic precision. Our thanks will never be enough for the unpredicted happiness their support has afforded us.

It is our great fortune to possess an archive of original, public-domain materials that allows us to select the best patterns of an era. We have been sincere and diligent in our efforts to include only materials that are in public domain.

Finally, thank you to the illustrators who spent their careers creating designs for us to stitch to life. So many of their names are lost to everyone except their families, or those who may remember working with them. It seems unlikely they imagined how enduring their work would prove to be. Our goal has always been to build recognition for the joy and delight these artists contributed to our lives, as well as the lives of millions throughout several generations. Please remember them when you admire vintage embroidery.

Brenna and Nori

Contents

Introduction

Perhaps no needlework is so infused with joy as the items we sew to welcome a baby into the world. We pour hope and love into every stitch, choosing designs that soothe, amuse, and delight.

During the last century, sewing for children developed into a decorative form that reflected the rapidly changing culture of childhood. Capturing the bedtime enchantment of fairy tales, lullabies, and sweet dreams, embroidered children's designs became the preserve of fanciful imagination.

Crib quilts and sheets featuring these designs were often the focus of nursery décor, and our sentimental attachment to them can begin at an early age. Embroidered crib quilts trace the rise and fall of a popular needlework phenomenon, advertised as art needlework and art embroidery by the companies that sold manufactured patterns and kits.

This decorative medium, with its roots in mass production, hasn't always been recognized for its artistic merits. However, it is widely loved by collectors who value its power to evoke a more tender time. This leisure activity, which has entertained thousands of women for a century, deserves a closer look.

Early Nursery Embroidery

Children's coverlets or small quilts have been made for centuries. Only in the last half of the nineteenth century did pre-stamped or manufactured embroidery designs become available. These designs could be quickly and easily embroidered in outline stitch, although chain and backstitch were sometimes used. This less-demanding technique did not replace extravagant eyelet, satin stitch, and lace work. Instead, it provided a new outlet for fancywork enthusiasts.

Compared to many fancywork projects that filled ladies' magazines in the 1880s, outline embroidery was a leisurely and casual pursuit. Once learned, this simple stitch quickly became fluid and efficient, allowing even detailed quilt blocks to be completed in just a few hours. Baby quilts from this era were often the result of putting an older sister's learning blocks to good use when the new baby arrived. Outline embroidery was a desirable decoration for items such as crib quilts, which would endure excessive use and frequent washing.

Both fanciful and simple designs adorned early embroidered quilts for children. Strawberries, ducks, and spiders, for example, might share the quilt with a cow jumping over the moon. Before the 1920s, coordinated sets of children's blocks were rare, and the majority were limited to favorite themes such as Mother Goose. From the beginning, however, outline embroidery themes were linked to images found in the growing market of publishing for children.

Recalling an idealized world of mid-nineteenth century childhood, Kate Greenaway's books for children had an immediate influence on the style of popular embroidery designs from the 1880s through the early 1900s. Needle-art companies quickly adapted Greenaway's drawings into a vast array of designs for everything from washstand "splashers" to crazy quilts. Combining striking realism with lighthearted themes, these motifs reflect dominant characteristics of late-Victorian children's items.

The booming business of children's publishing fed a steady stream of nursery projects to ladies' periodicals and advertising premiums in

Early Nursery Embroidery

the first decades of the twentieth century. Celebrity illustrators helped magazines and pattern publishers compete for readers. Bertha Corbett's Sunbonnet Babies were adapted to embroidery as quickly as Kate Greenaway's children had been, and even appeared in foreign-language periodicals such as *Deutsche Haus Frau*. Artist Grace Wiederseim Drayton, creator of the Campbell's Kids and Dolly Dingle, treated readers of the *Ladies' Home Journal* to an exclusive series of embroidery motifs for nursery linens, crib sheets, and towels. Characters like Buster Brown and Palmer Cox's Brownies were equally popular subjects in their day, enhancing tinted nursery pillows finished with embroidery.

The embroidered nursery quilt most recognized today was defined during the 1920s. The flourishing economy nourished manufacturers of stamped embroidery patterns and kits. Needlework catalogs were filled with novel projects. With children as the target audience, these projects frequently were tinted with soft, yet vibrant colors. Mother Goose continued to be popular, while nursery animals, teddy bears, and other themes appeared in coordinated projects including curtains, quilts, and matching toys.

The delightful designs of Ruby McKim were quite possibly the most important components in popularizing embroidered quilts. Beginning in the mid-1920s, her prolific and prodigious imagination produced dozens of innovative outline embroidery patterns. Christmas, farm life, toys, and dozens of other themes found unique expression through McKim's newspaper pattern column and the pages of her catalog. Though not always meant exclusively for children, her restrained yet whimsical style fit perfectly into the nurseries of the late 1920s and the 1930s.

Tinted coverlets enjoyed their strongest vogue from the mid-1920s until shortly after World War II. Mimicking the look of appliqué without its time-consuming work, pre-tinted kits were quickly finished with the easiest possible embroidery. A plain running stitch could even be used on these projects. Such crib sheets were seldom, if ever, quilted and could be purchased in designs for infants to young school children. Washed in vivid color like a professionally painted coloring book, tinted crib sheets point clearly to the strong relationship between children's book illustrations and the development of embroidery for the nursery.

After the war, the nursery's world was filled with slick colors of the modern age. Many small embroidery pattern companies had succumbed to the rationing and shortages of the war effort. Remaining companies featured more refined, professionally cartooned designs that matched the illustrative style of educational books. Cowboys and ballerinas filled bedrooms across the country. Howdy Doody and Walt Disney's entire crew were available for embroidery.

With their large designs, pre-stamped crib quilts took a front seat to home-stamped and pieced baby quilts. It was on projects like these that many baby boomers took their first stitches. Despite the lagging popularity of stamped embroidery in the late 1960s and 1970s, stamped crib quilts continued to find an audience, always following in the trends of children's illustrations.

Collector's Trivia

Today, nostalgia for early embroidery designs fuels an active collectible market in both vintage patterns and finished work. The market for nursery linens has steadily increased in the last several years. Items in mint to excellent condition are rare because children wore out most of their possessions, even those used exclusively for bedtime. Sentiment keeps many people from parting with childhood items, which enhances the sellers' market.

Determining the age on stamped embroidered textiles is tricky. Even experienced collectors can miscalculate the vintage of embroidered items. This is caused partly by the longevity of popular patterns. Pattern companies often sold the same patterns for 20 years or more. Nursery linens are especially vulnerable to this consideration

An experienced textile conservator can distinguish age from the fabric weave and apparent content, but these characteristics can be subtle to the hobbyist. A few basic guidelines for determining the age of vintage crib quilts and sheets follow.

Assume 1930 or later. Embroidered blocks from after the war comprise the bulk of vintage crib quilts. Crib sheets and quilts from the 1920s and earlier are more unusual. Those in excellent condition are even more rare.

Tinted treasure. Tinted nursery items, particularly crib sheets, are the most collectible and, therefore, the most costly. Large-scale, commercial tinting of crib sheets was short-lived. In this category, nursery items featuring military themes from the war years get the top dollar.

Values in pink and blue. Embroidered blocks for nursery quilts, circa 1945 to 1955, are by contrast reasonably plentiful and affordable. Sets of eight to ten blocks can be found for $1.00 to $1.50 per block.

Age is in the eyes. Big eyes, long eyelashes, and pudgy cheeks are the typical illustration style on nursery patterns from the late 1930s on. This style reflected the tremendous influence of Walt Disney and other animators on children's consumables. The style of the eyes is an excellent indication of pattern age, because the eyes were often the only part of a pattern to be revamped to extend its shelf life.

Know your style. Earlier than 1940, adorable animals displayed distinctive styles. Look for exaggerated or simplistic shapes typical of the 1920s and 1930s. Highly realistic or slightly naive figures characterized turn-of-the-century and earlier styles. If the style reminds you of a classic cartoon, think 1940s or later.

Look at the pictures. Children's picture books or coloring books provide great clues to the styles typically seen in nursery embroidery. They help develop a feeling for the look of different decades. Overall, vintage children's books are affordable, unless fine condition is preferred over fair condition.

Catalog clues. If you consider collecting and investing in nursery quilts, a few ladies' magazines and embroidery catalogs from the era of interest are helpful. These publications clearly illustrate what's typical for a given time frame.

Collector's Trivia

Trust your intuition. Don't be afraid to second guess the date given by a dealer. There is limited documentation to base an appraisal on most popular vintage linens. The best way to find a bargain is to know the era you love better than a dealer does.

Expect contradictions. It's not unusual to find redwork nursery quilts with blocks that were embroidered 20 years apart. Learning blocks from one generation were sometimes combined with more experienced work completed later, or by a different person. The effect can be jarring. One of our favorite finds combined crudely embroidered redwork patterns from the 1880s with feedsack sashing and acrylic yarn.

Expect exceptions. Some pattern companies were noted for the realism of their designs throughout the decades, even when the trend was to stylize. Joseph Walker patterns are a good example of this. Others, like McCalls, featured some highly stylized designs from the beginning.

Shop savvy on-line. Tried-and-true collectors' haunts, such as flea markets, antique malls, and estate auctions, have expanded to include on-line auctions. The advantages of shopping on-line have produced a dramatic change in the availability and prices of collectible linens.

Beginning collectors can use on-line auctions to educate themselves about the prevailing market for items of interest by viewing completed auction histories. Textile descriptions should clearly state areas of wear and staining. While it is your responsibility to ask questions about an item, a good on-line dealer who is selling something worth the price should offer a refund if it is not as described.

Tinting Tips

The smooth, shaded color that collectors love on tinted antique baby items originates from paints applied in a professional setting. With a little practice, however, it is possible to get the same look using modern fabric paints.

Our favorite technique involves a little freezer paper stencil and a 1" stencil brush. Load the stencil brush with a dab of paint, then vigorously bounce it against a paper plate at least a dozen times. Don't worry if it seems that too much paint is coming off; there is plenty in the brush. Test on a paper towel by lightly dabbing or stroking the brush. Apply the paint lightly to the fabric with a gentle pouncing motion. A delicate touch is the key. Apply the color to the fabric lightly, then deepen as desired to add shading. Avoid overloading your brush with too much paint. Paint a practice block or two to make sure you achieve the look you want. Where tinted areas touch, apply the light color first and allow it to dry before applying the darker color. Drying can be hastened with an iron.

Crayon, which is an old-fashioned way of coloring quilt blocks, is regaining popularity. It is wonderfully easy to apply; however, the color can fade when washed repeatedly, even when set with salt. To help preserve the color, wash only in cold water and never scrub directly on the colored areas. For the smoothest application of color, use the blunt end of the crayon with the edge sanded a bit. Keep the darkest shading near the edge of the pattern for a dimensional effect.

Always trace your design first, using a permanent ink pen. It's easier to match your stencil to the traced pattern than vice versa.

Paint-tinted block before embroidery.

Embroidered paint-tinted block.

Greenaway Crossing

Inspired by both daily life and nostalgic sentiment, early embroidered children's quilts were windows into young life at the turn of the twentieth century. Scenes of children at the seashore were most often found on redwork splashers, while children with flowers were favorites for every kind of redwork item, including quilt blocks.

In the antique illustrations by Kate Greenaway, an idealized view of carefree childhood is captured. Paint books, the earliest versions of coloring books, featured dozens of illustrations like these, usually adapting themes from advertising art, popular children's books, and famous illustrators. Parents were enticed to buy paint books for budding artists at home. It didn't take women long to realize that illustrations from these books were perfectly adaptable to embroidery designs. Letters sharing this "hint for needleworkers" appeared early in the twentieth century in many fancywork columns.

Greenaway Crossing

Embroidered Childhood Memories – *Brenna Hopkins & Nori Koenig*

Greenaway Crossing

Greenaway Crossing

Embroidered Childhood Memories – *Brenna Hopkins & Nori Koenig*

Greenaway Crossing

Greenaway Crossing

Embroidered Childhood Memories – *Brenna Hopkins & Nori Koenig*

Greenaway Crossing

Greenaway Crossing

Embroidered Childhood Memories – *Brenna Hopkins & Nori Koenig*

Greenaway Crossing

Greenaway Crossing

Embroidered Childhood Memories – *Brenna Hopkins & Nori Koenig*

Ladies Art Letters

The Ladies Art Company is well known among quilters for the hundreds of elaborate patchwork patterns it published beginning in the late Victorian era. Its contribution to redwork's popularity is becoming better known, too.

Redwork patterns listed originally by the Ladies Art Company appeared as subscription premiums in popular ladies' magazines. Ladies Art offered several dozen redwork designs in a mid-1890s catalog, including the Sunbonnet Baby patterns based on the Bernhardt Wall postcards, and an unusual sprinting Santa Claus.

Elaborate alphabets, which often told a story using rhyme, were tremendously popular themes for children's picture and paint books in the early 1900s. Suggestions to use alphabet patterns for cloth baby books appeared in project columns of the *Modern Priscilla* and *Ladies' Home Journal* magazines.

Ladies Art Letters

Embroidered Childhood Memories – *Brenna Hopkins & Nori Koenig*

Ladies Art Letters

Ladies Art Letters

Embroidered Childhood Memories – *Brenna Hopkins & Nori Koenig*

Sunbonnet Babies

At the turn of the twentieth century, several artists illustrated sunbonnet figures. Bertha Corbett's designs proved to be the most enduring because of her ability to capture childhood's timeless simplicity. Although the babies occasionally appeared in endorsements, Bertha Corbett's work remained largely her own, and her sunbonnets succeeded as uniquely charming storybook characters.

Though other sunbonnet-style patterns were available as early as the 1890s, the irrepressible Molly and May appeared in commercially manufactured embroidery patterns around the turn of the twentieth century. The Sunbonnet Alphabet and Sunbonnet Seasons were among the most popular of these patterns. The Sunbonnet Babies also appeared in school primers, no doubt delighting children lucky enough to learn to read with Molly and May.

Sunbonnet Babies

Embroidered Childhood Memories – *Brenna Hopkins & Nori Koenig*

Sunbonnet Babies

Sunbonnet Babies

Embroidered Childhood Memories – *Brenna Hopkins & Nori Koenig*

Sunbonnet Babies

Sunbonnet Babies

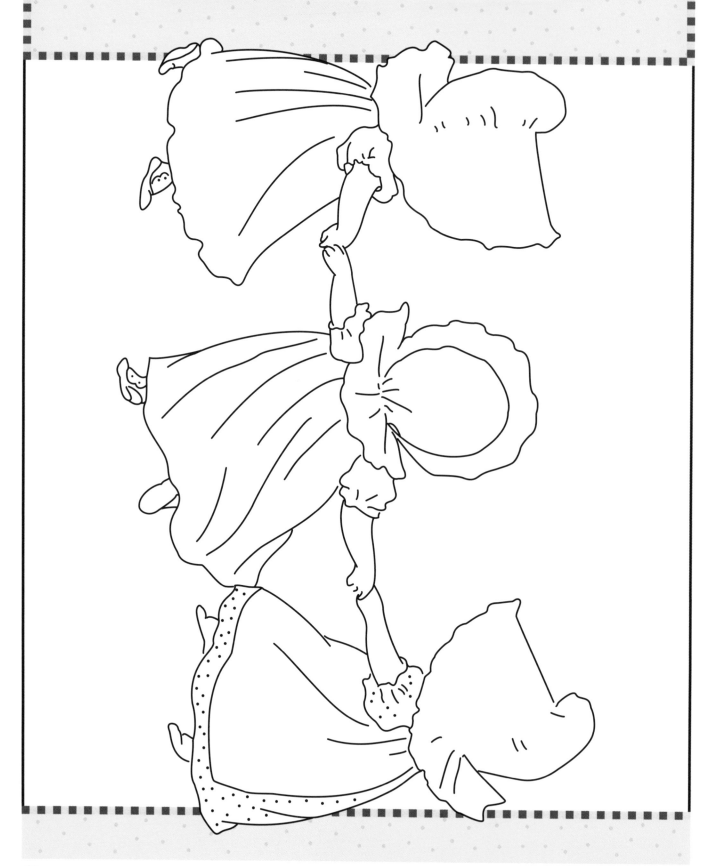

Embroidered Childhood Memories – *Brenna Hopkins & Nori Koenig*

Sunbonnet Babies

Sunbonnet Babies

Embroidered Childhood Memories – *Brenna Hopkins & Nori Koenig*

Tip Top Toddlers

At once playful and earnest, these babies display genteel good manners in up-to-the minute children's clothing, circa 1923. It's a style unique to the decade, delicately feminine, yet lighthearted and fun.

It's no coincidence that these figures are so beautiful. The illustrators creating this influential style were women artists, bringing tremendous skill and special feeling to their portrayals of children. The carefree, whimsical atmosphere of their fashion drawings was worthy of any picture book, and probably as important to selling clothing patterns as the design of the clothes themselves. The work of these illustrators can often be found in 1920s picture and school books, though unfortunately much of it was unsigned.

Tip Top Toddlers

Embroidered Childhood Memories – *Brenna Hopkins & Nori Koenig*

Tip Top Toddlers

Tip Top Toddlers

Embroidered Childhood Memories – *Brenna Hopkins & Nori Koenig*

Tip Top Toddlers

Tip Top Toddlers

Embroidered Childhood Memories – *Brenna Hopkins & Nori Koenig*

Tip Top Toddlers

Tip Top Toddlers

Embroidered Childhood Memories – Brenna Hopkins & Nori Koenig

Tip Top Toddlers

Tip Top Toddlers

Embroidered Childhood Memories – *Brenna Hopkins & Nori Koenig*

Tip Top Toddlers

Tip Top Toddlers

Embroidered Childhood Memories – *Brenna Hopkins & Nori Koenig*

Tip Top Toddlers

Tip Top Toddlers

Embroidered Childhood Memories – *Brenna Hopkins & Nori Koenig*

Tip Top Toddlers

Tip Top Toddlers

Tip Top Toddlers

Tip Top Toddlers

Embroidered Childhood Memories – *Brenna Hopkins & Nori Koenig*

Tip Top Toddlers

Tip Top Toddlers

Embroidered Childhood Memories – *Brenna Hopkins & Nori Koenig*

Tip Top Toddlers

Tip Top Toddlers

Tip Top Toddlers

Tip Top Toddlers

Embroidered Childhood Memories – *Brenna Hopkins & Nori Koenig*

Tip Top Toddlers

Tip Top Toddlers

Embroidered Childhood Memories – *Brenna Hopkins & Nori Koenig*

Tip Top Toddlers

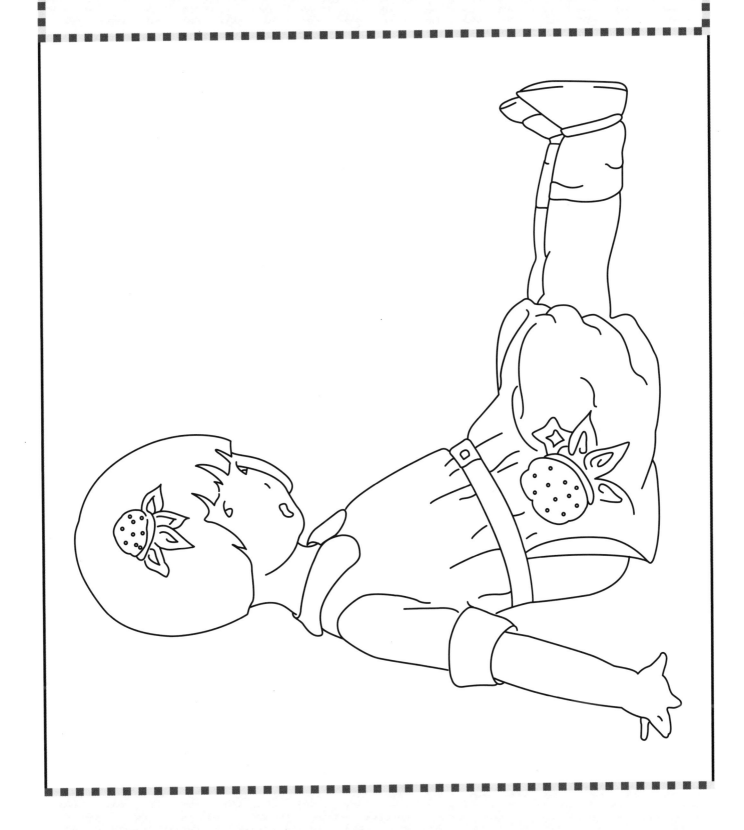

Tip Top Toddlers

Embroidered Childhood Memories – *Brenna Hopkins & Nori Koenig*

Coloring Book Alphabet
Deco Era

oloring books have inspired nursery embroidery patterns since the early 1900s. Whimsical subjects from coloring books appealed to children, and their simplified outlines made them perfect for embroidery.

Although popular throughout the 1920s, coloring books like the one that inspired the Deco Era blocks began their greatest period of popularity in the late 1930s. Dozens of titles were published every year by the large coloring book companies, each with a style distinctly its own. The stylized Art Deco toys and characters of this alphabet fit perfectly into a nursery of the mid-1930s.

Coloring Book Alphabet
Deco Era

Embroidered Childhood Memories – *Brenna Hopkins & Nori Koenig*

Coloring Book Alphabet
Deco Era

Coloring Book Alphabet

Deco Era

Embroidered Childhood Memories – Brenna Hopkins & Nori Koenig

Coloring Book Alphabet
Deco Era

Coloring Book Alphabet
Deco Era

Coloring Book Alphabet
Deco Era

Coloring Book Alphabet
Deco Era

Embroidered Childhood Memories – *Brenna Hopkins & Nori Koenig*

Coloring Book Alphabet
Deco Era

Coloring Book Alphabet
Deco Era

Embroidered Childhood Memories – Brenna Hopkins & Nori Koenig

Coloring Book Alphabet
Deco Era

Coloring Book Alphabet
Deco Era

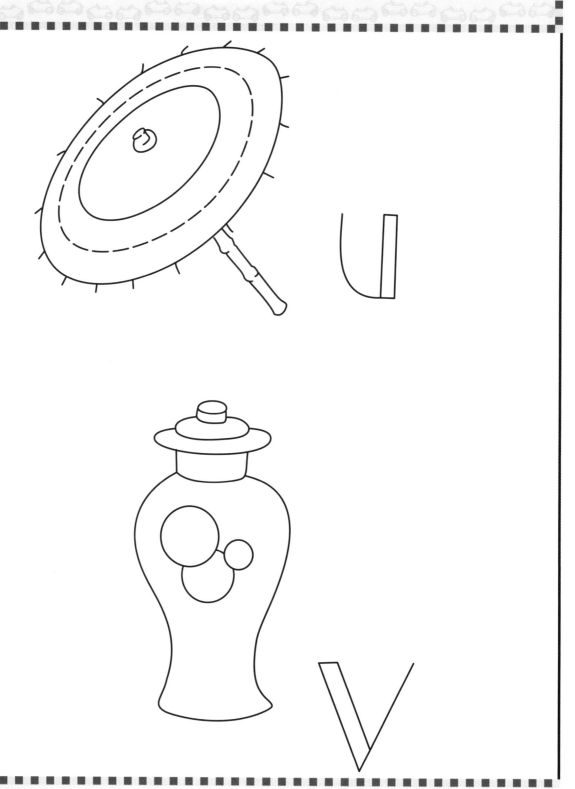

Embroidered Childhood Memories – *Brenna Hopkins & Nori Koenig*

Coloring Book Alphabet
Deco Era

Coloring Book Alphabet
Deco Era

Embroidered Childhood Memories – *Brenna Hopkins & Nori Koenig*

Coloring Book Alphabet
Eisenhower Era

In the years immediately following World War II, exuberantly colored embroidery patterns flooded the market. Nurseries and children's items were bright with technicolor duckies and lambs, chasing away dreary memories of sacrifice for the war effort. Children's clothes, pictures, and school books sang with this brilliant color, celebrating the prosperous new life families envisioned.

As elementary as Dick and Jane, the easy shapes of these alphabet figures are inspired by post-war children's readers. Touches of fabric paint and black outlining can add typical 1940s style to the patterns (see Tinting Tips, page 10). The distinctive simplicity of the illustrations marks their vintage, which is in contrast to the elaborate realism of late Victorian nursery embroidery. However, they are more realistic than the stylized Art Deco of the 1920s and 1930s.

Coloring Book Alphabet

Eisenhower Era

A a

B b

C c

D d

Embroidered Childhood Memories – Brenna Hopkins & Nori Koenig

Coloring Book Alphabet

Eisenhower Era

Ee Ff

Gg Hh

Coloring Book Alphabet

Eisenhower Era

Embroidered Childhood Memories – *Brenna Hopkins & Nori Koenig*

Coloring Book Alphabet

Eisenhower Era

M m

N n

O o

P p

Coloring Book Alphabet

Eisenhower Era

Coloring Book Alphabet

Eisenhower Era

Coloring Book Alphabet

Eisenhower Era

Embroidered Childhood Memories – Brenna Hopkins & Nori Koenig

Bedtime Babies

Influenced by the optimism and expansion of post-war America, nurseries were whimsically cheerful. Refined looks and professional design appear in marked contrast to the homespun images seen in earlier embroidered nursery items. The circular embroidery format here suggests the modern look prevailing throughout post-war homes.

Taking their cue from Walt Disney and Warner Brothers, pattern makers developed the expressive eyes and long lashes that distinguish children's patterns from this era. The range of expression created from just a few stitches is masterful.

As the pace of post-war life quickened, busy young mothers seemed to have had less time for leisure needlework. Pre-stamped goods and catalog color charts from companies such as Vogart, American Thread, Aunt Ellen's, and Aunt Martha's offered variety and convenience probably not matched since the 1920s. Embroidered touches decorated everything from bibs and booties to adorable toys.

Bedtime Babies

Bedtime Babies

Bedtime Babies

Embroidered Childhood Memories – *Brenna Hopkins & Nori Koenig*

Bedtime Babies

Bedtime Babies

Embroidered Childhood Memories – *Brenna Hopkins & Nori Koenig*

Child's Play

Now prized as heirlooms, penny-square quilts often served to teach embroidery to young girls. As a girl's collection of embroidered muslin blocks grew, so did her quilt top. Personal touches and changing tastes guaranteed that each quilt would be utterly unique. This evident personal involvement in quilt design makes penny-square quilts especially satisfying to collect.

Recent research has helped to identify the enormous quantity of commercially available redwork patterns from the late nineteenth century. Dozens of stamped designs could once be bought almost anywhere that sold thread. Creating designs from coloring book pictures or other sources was undeniably popular, as a way to add further self expression to the quilt. Detailed designs such as these were marketed to older, more experienced embroiderers; however, they fit nicely with the simpler patterns a girl might choose as a beginner.

Child's Play

Embroidered Childhood Memories – *Brenna Hopkins & Nori Koenig*

Child's Play

Child's Play

Embroidered Childhood Memories – *Brenna Hopkins & Nori Koenig*

Child's Play

Child's Play

Embroidered Childhood Memories – *Brenna Hopkins & Nori Koenig*

Child's Play

Other AQS Books

This is only a small selection of the books available from the American Quilter's Society. AQS books are known worldwide for timely topics, clear writing, beautiful color photos, and accurate illustrations and patterns. The following books are available from your local bookseller, quilt shop, or public library.

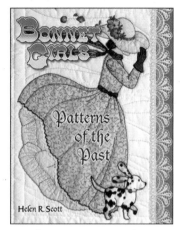

#5763   us$21.95

#6002   us$15.95

#6077   us$24.95

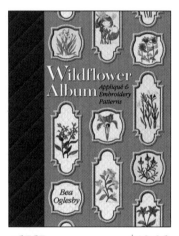

#5757   us$19.95

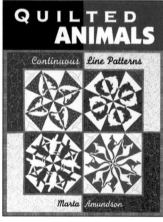

#6071   us$22.95

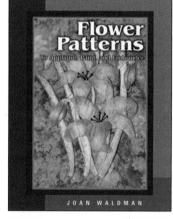

#5238   us$19.95

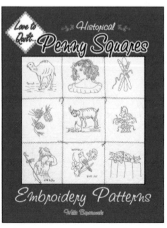

#4753   us$12.95

#5849   us$21.95

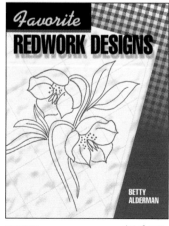

#5331   us$16.95

Look for these books nationally or call 1-800-626-5420